Butterflies, Bears, and Other Poems for Children

Written and Illustrated by

Patricia Herber

LitFire LLC
1-800-511-9787
www.litfirepublishing.com
order@litfirepublishing.com

Contents

I am dedicating my ***Butterflies, Bears, and Other Poems for Children*** anthology to my precious grandchildren – Kyleigh, Bryce, Bre, Bentley, Yardley, and Alyssa May.

Special thanks to my daughter Amy, son Ryan, and husband Larry for their love, support, and encouragement through this exciting adventure of writing, illustrating, and publishing a book.

Bear Cubs

Bear cubs –
I like them.

Because they're cute.
Because they're soft and cuddly.
Because they have paws and climb trees.
Because they're curious.
Because they follow their mamas around.
Because they eat ants and honey.
Because sometimes bees chase after them.
Because… sometimes they get into trouble.

Because. That's why!

I like bear cubs.

Teddy Bears

A teddy bear is your special friend,
No matter if you're a girl or a boy.
You can tell secrets to your bear
'Cause he's probably your favorite toy.

Teddy bears come in all shapes and sizes,
All different colors too;
Their fur can be shaggy, curly, or straight,
Some real old – some new

You can read stories to your Teddy,
You can share some milk and cookies.
You can hold your teddy when you're scared.
And when you're sick, or have scraped knees.

You can dress your Teddy in pajamas
When you get tucked into bed at night.
You can tell your Teddy how your day went,
You can hug him and snuggle up tight.

Toy bears are named for President Teddy Roosevelt
Whose friends caught a bear cub and tied it to a tree.
When the President saw what they had done,
He told them to set the little cub free.

Butterflies

I love butterfly dresses.
Butterfly socks
Butterfly books
Butterfly clocks
Butterfly houses
Butterfly skies
Butterflies flitting in front of my eyes
While others like cats or boats with a sail,
I'd rather have a yellow swallowtail.

Some Girls Like...

Cheerleading, basketball
Books and DVDs
Ice skating, volleyball
Soccer and CDs

Make up and dressing up
Perfume and rings
Cocker Spaniel pups
And dainty frilly things

Jumping rope, knitting
Chocolate ice cream cones
Shopping, babysitting
Purple telephones

Secrets, friends, and TV shows
Making lots of noise
Earrings, bows, and panty hose
And yes, even boys

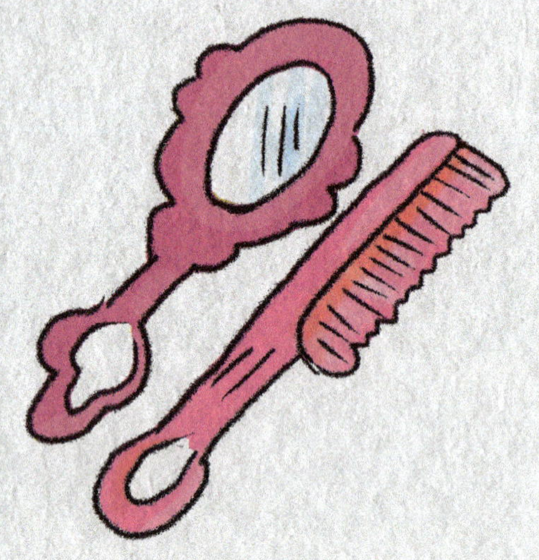

Some Boys Like...

Soccer and football
Cars, trucks, and trains
Wrestling and basketball
Dinosaurs, airplanes

Lizards and snakes
Fish and tadpoles
Thick chocolate shakes
Old swimming holes

Video games, their mothers
Yummy cakes and pies
Fighting with their brothers
Hanging with the guys

Hot dogs and baseballs
Ice cream with swirls
Race cars and phone calls
And yes, even girls

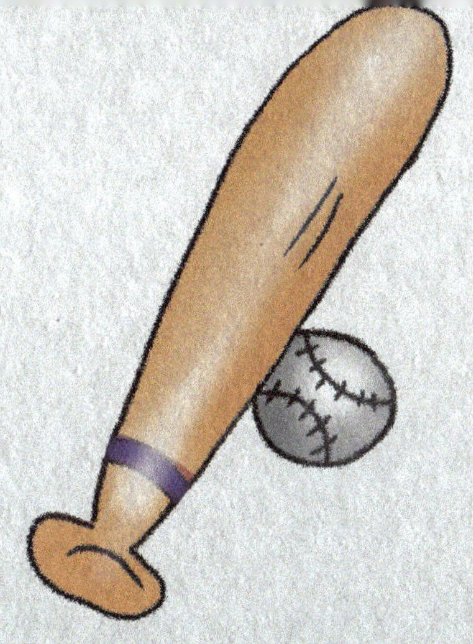

Rhymes

I learned about rhymes
And rhymes are lots of fun.
You can make about eight new words
That started out as one.

Start with a word like **bat**.
Turn the **b** to a **c**.
Now the new word is **cat**,
As you can plainly see.

If you change the **c** to **f**
You get the new word **fat**.
If you change it to an **h**
The new word is now **hat**.

Think of all the new words
You can read in a short time
Like **mat**, **rat**, **sat**, and **that**
Now that you know how to rhyme.

Reading a Book

Some people don't like to read books.
Why, I cannot say.
'Cause since I learned how to read,
I'm reading every day.

First, and most important,
I think reading's fun.
Once you know how to do it,
The fun's just begun!

You can travel to far away places,
You can solve a mystery,
You can read about all kinds of people,
Have an adventure at sea.

There are so many things
You can learn from a book
If you only pick one up
And just take a look.

Monkey

I'd like to be a monkey
Swinging from a tree,
Yelling to my brother, "You can't catch me!"

I'd like to be a monkey
Eating a banana,
Sharing it at breakfast with my sister Hannah.

I'd like to be a monkey
On a green jungle vine,
Playing in a playground, practically all mine.

I'd like to be a monkey
Taking a nap,
Snoozing in my Mama's warm and comfy lap.

Elephant Parts

I think elephants have
big feet so they can hide
marbles between their toes.

I think elephants have
tails that look like those tassels
that hang from caps when people graduate.
I think elephants have trunks that are really dandy.
They come in handy

for picking up food
for smelling
for pushing trees over

for getting a drink
for taking a shower

And,

I think elephants have
big floppy ears that
they use to fan themselves dry

Because...
They don't have any towels!

Puppy

I was turning eight that year
And Mother said I could
Get a puppy for my birthday
'Cause I was kind and good.

We went to the pet shop
Just to take a look…
It was only five minutes –
That was all it took.

I spied a Cocker Spaniel puppy
That was just the right size
With curly long ears
And big black eyes.

It had taffy-colored fur
And a little stumped tail.
I just had to know
It if was still for sale.

I named the dog Taffy.
We're never apart.
We're best friends forever.
She's close to my heart.

Babies

A baby dog is a puppy.
A baby seal's a pup too.
A baby duck's a duckling,
A joey's a young kangaroo.

A newborn cat is a kitten.
A baby deer is a fawn.
Do you think, that when they're tired,
They like to curl up and yawn?

Baby lions, bears, and tigers,
I know, are all called cubs.
Do you think they all eat honey,
And sometimes get belly-rubs?

A baby elephant's a calf.
An infant cow is too.
So is a newborn hippo
And a young whale, brand new

An eaglet's a baby eagle.
A piglet's a tiny pig.
And a tadpole becomes a frog
When it starts to grow big.

A baby goat is a kid.
I just learned something new.
And I think **that** is funny,
Because I'm a kid too!

Mixed-up Mother Goose

"Mommy, could you read to me before I go to bed?"
Mother smiled warmly, and this is what she said,
"I'll read **Mother Goose** to you from the first page to the last,
but it's way past bedtime, so I'm going to read it fast."

Little Sophie yawned several times,
then drifted off to sleep, dreaming of nursery rhymes.

Georgie Porgie, pudding and pie,
Kissed Bo-Peep and made her cry.
Mary had some little lambs and can't tell where to find them,
Leave them alone and they'll come home with Little Boy Blue behind them.
Little Boy Blue come blow your horn,
Peter Pumpkin's in the meadow, Jack-be-Nimble's in the corn.
Jack and Jill went up the hill to fetch a pail of water.
Jack fell down and broke his crown and Humpty Dumpty came tumbling after.

With that, little Sophie sat upright in her bed,
'Cause the characters from **Mother Goose** were mixed up in her head.

Do You Remember...

A girl named Cinderella, her
   stepmom, and stepsisters
Whose fairy godmother made
   her a ball gown and glass slippers

A tasty gingerbread boy who
   was outsmarted, and is gone forever
Because he was eaten by a fox who
   was sly and clever

A puppet named Pinocchio who
   grew donkey ears and a tail
Then became a real boy after he
   saved Gepetto from a whale

A donkey, cat, dog, and a rooster
   who used their voices
To chase robbers from a house
   by making scary noises

A shoemaker who made clothes for
   two tiny elves
Because they helped him make
   shoes to sell on his shelves

People in a village who add
   vegetables to stone soup
Because they get tricked into
   doing it by the king's troops

Three pigs who built homes of
   bricks, straws, and sticks
And a wolf who couldn't blow
   down the house of bricks

A girl named Goldilocks who ate
   Little Bear's porridge one day,
Broke his chair, slept in his bed,
   and was frightened away.

Naming the Animals

If the naming of the zoo animals
   was left up to me,
I would choose their names
   and here's what they'd be:

Jenny Giraffe, Sophie Seal,
   Zelda Zebra, Wally Walrus
Bozo Bear, Tex Tiger,
   Pete Peacock, Rosie Rhinoceros

Ellie Elephant, Lyle Crocodile,
   Alex Alligator, Benny Buffalo
Morris Moose, Kyle Kangaroo,
   Anthony Antelope, and Hilda Hippo

Elmer Eagle, Carla Camel,
   Tootsie Turtle, Dolly Donkey
Polly Parrot, Ollie Ostrich,
   Daphne Duck, and Marvin Monkey

I guess it doesn't matter
   if they even have a name;
If you give them some attention,
   they'll like you just the same.

First Day of School

Mommy is upset 'cause she can't say "goodbye,"
But I'm real brave and I'm not gonna cry.
Riding on the bus can be really quite cool
When you're five years old and headed off to school.
I'm so excited! I don't want to be late,
So hurry up! It's half past eight.
I want to meet my teacher and see where I sit.

I want to read books and play a little bit.
Now get on the bus and take your seat
'Cause I think school is gonna be neat.

What Did You Learn Today?

When we get together for supper
My family, as a rule,
Asks each other how their day went
And what I learned that day at school.

I usually tell them
When I learn something new,
And I get quite excited
When it's cool and fun, too.

Like **Roy G. Biv** in Science
Who's not a man, but a trick
To recall the rainbow's colors
In a way that's neat and quick.

Roy is red, orange, yellow
G. is the color green
Biv is blue, indigo, violet
Now, <u>that</u> is keen!

My Mom and Dad were impressed by it,
And my big sister was, too.
She even said, "Thank you," to me
For teaching her something new.

Monarch Queen

We did a lesson in our classroom
That was a mystery to me.
We watched a caterpillar change to a butterfly
Which was a miracle to see.

At first we put some milkweed leaves
Into a clear glass jar,
And a tiny egg on the leaf
Became a caterpillar.

The worm ate through the juicy leaves
And got fatter every day,
Then attached herself to a leaf
By hanging in a **J**.

Next, she wiggled her body
And curled up into a small green shell.
This was called a "chrysalis,"
And it protected her very well.

A week later she fell out of the shell
And I thought that I would cry.
She was no longer a worm
But a beautiful butterfly!

Johnny Appleseed

Have you heard of Johnny Appleseed, the traveling man,
Who walked across the country with seeds and a plan?
Johnny planted the seeds wherever he'd go –
Pretty soon, apple trees started to grow.
Wherever he went, people knew him by name
For his kind reputation had given him fame.
He befriended the animals – deer, bear, and rabbits,
He respected their homes and learned their habits.
He slept under the stars, used the grass for his bed,
And walked across the states with a pot on his head.
With that pot on his head, he was funny-looking,
But as you can guess, he used it for cooking.
Now, thanks to Johnny, apples grow in many places
And apple pies do put big smiles on people's faces!

18

Fireman

Although he may look scary
When he wears the breathing mask,
A fireman is your special friend
'Cause he does a special task.

Whenever the alarm goes off
You can hear the fire chief shout.
The men get suited up real fast
Just as the truck's pulling out.

When they get to a house that's on fire
They always check inside.
It's important that they do that
'Cause sometimes children hide.

With their long ladders and hoses,
Water and special foam,
The firemen make sure the fire's out
Before the trucks go home.

Firemen don't just fight fires,
They help at car accidents too;
Sometimes they rescue cats in trees –
There's so much that they do.

Halloween Party

I went to a Halloween party.
All of my friends were there.
A witch, a ghost, and a vampire,
A skeleton on a chair.

A robot, a nurse, and a doctor
Were laughing and drinking milkshakes.
A fireman, a pirate, and a mermaid
Were talking and eating cupcakes.

A sailor, a wolf, and a waitress
Were dancing and having fun.
A fat clown and a ballerina
Sat next to a praying nun.

I was glad everyone wore a costume.
The ghost scared me, and loudly said , "Boo!"
But the trouble with a costume party
Is that nobody knows who's who!

Poor Tom Turkey

The turkey's in the oven.
It smells really good.
From Thanksgivings past,
I knew that it would.

I especially like Thanksgiving.
It's family time for me,
But I always feel sorry
For the poor turkey.

Last week I saw him
Struttin' around the farm.
Why would anybody
Want to do him harm?

Plump and round and friendly,
Tom Turkey had no inkling
That he would be the main dish
At our family Thanksgiving.

I wish I could have spared him
From his awful fate,
But I couldn't persuade Grandpa,
And now it's too late.

Tom Turkey's in the oven
Turning golden brown.
I know I should be thankful,
But I can only frown.

Ready for Christmas

The month of December brings an end to the year,
The magic of Christmas, love, and good cheer.
It's always a job to untangle the lights,
To get them all working, shiny and bright.
The tree is decorated with tinsel and bows;
At the top sits a beautiful star all a-glow.
The house is all festive from ceiling to floor,
The Christmas cards mailed, the wreath hung on the door.
The cookies are baked, fresh from the oven –
All kinds and shapes – we counted six dozen.
Christmas Eve has arrived, and we're all set.
This promises to be our best Christmas yet!

Snowy Day Friend

Did you wish you had a friend when you went out to play?
Did you ever build a snowman on a cold and snowy day?

If you need some advice, I'll tell you what to do,
And then, when you're lonely, you'll have a friend, too!

First, get the snow and pack it real tight,
Roll it into balls, and stack them up right.
The biggest ball's the body, the belly's in the middle,
The ball on top's the head, which of course, you know, is little.
You can wrap a scarf around the neck, add earmuffs or a hat,
Use branches for the arms, or something like that.
Try large buttons for the eyes, a carrot for the nose,
Stones to make a mouth – almost anything goes.
When you shape the mouth be sure to form a smile,
"Cause a smile's always happy, and in a little while...

You'll find that you're not lonely on this cold and snowy day,
Because you made a friend when you went out to play.

Groundhog Day

I'm a plump and husky groundhog
As you can plainly see,
And the 2nd day in February
Is a special day for me.

I must predict the weather.
The job was made for me.
Will it snow, or flowers grow?
What's it gonna be?

My critter instincts tell me
It's time for me to wake.
The sun will determine
The decision that I make.

If the sun is shining brightly
And my shadow's on the ground,
I run back to my burrow
To where I can't be found.

What that means for humans
Is simple as can be –
Six more weeks of Winter weather,
Six more weeks of sleep for me.

But...

If I don't see my shadow,
Then Spring is on its way.
I stay outside and hunt for food
And run and dig and play.

Teeth

Did you ever stop to wonder
Why people have teeth?
They help you talk, help you smile,
And especially help you eat.

You need to visit the dentist,
Floss and brush everyday.
If you don't take care of them
They're going to decay.

Then you'll get cavities –
Holes and pain in your teeth.
The dentist will need to fill them
To give you some relief.

Sometimes teeth become crooked
And don't grow in right.
Then you can get braces
To help fix your bite.

Think about some of the animals
Living at the zoo.
Do you think they'd have nicer smiles
If they had braces too?

Secret Valentine

I received a pretty valentine
that someone sent to me.
Since I don't know who it's from,
it sure is a mystery.
The card is simply lovely
with a pink heart at the base
and a decorated border of white and frilly lace.

Inside there is a message
for only me to see –
a note of admiration, especially for me.
It says that someone loves me,
but he's too shy to say,
So his love remains a secret
for at least another day.

Dinosaurs

In school I learned about T-Rex, who was a tyrant king.
He killed other dinosaurs, and was the meanest thing.
He had large back legs but real short front arms
That he used to attack others to try to do them harm.
Since his teeth were sharp and pointy and they shred the meat he tore,
He was called a meat-eater, or a Carnivore.

One of T-Rex's enemies was the Brontosaurus
Who had a very long neck, and was simply enormous.
Nicknamed "thunder lizard", he made thunder sounds when he walked;
But ran to water for safety, when, by T-Rex he was stalked.
Since his teeth were flat and straight, he ate vines, and more.
He was called a plant-eater, or a herbivore.

Another dinosaur was the mighty Stegosaurus
Who scientists believe, left fossil prints for us.
He had bony spikes and plates down his tail and his back
That he used for protection when he was under attack.
I loved learning about these beasts of long ago
And I really wish they still lived today, you know.

Lucky Leprechaun

I went for a walk one morn' in a field of shamrock green
And chanced upon a leprechaun over by a stream.
He was sitting on a toadstool with a pot of gold
In an emerald green suit that was tattered and old.
He was the tiniest elf I ever did see,
For he looked to be only about two feet, three.

He seemed very happy, so I took a closer peek.
I saw two pointy ears and a dimple on his cheek.
He told me he was lucky, and with a nod of his head,
Gave me a four-leaf clover he had found in the bed.
He told me to place it inside of my shoe;
That it would work like magic, and I'd be lucky too.

Barnyard Morning

At 5 o'clock in the morning
Rex Rooster crows to Hattie Hen
Who clucks to her baby chicks
To eat the corn outside the pen.

Next big old Barney Bull
Moos to Clara Cow.
She moos to little calf
To drink his breakfast now.

Then mother Nanny Goat
Bleats to husband Bill.
He baas to their seven kids
To eat the grass up on the hill.

Soon spotted Sally Sow
Oinks to Ben the Boar
Who guides the tiny piglets
To the slop by the door.

Finally darling Doris Duck
Quacks to Donald Drake.
"Time to feed the ducklings, dear,
Down by the lake."

Coloring Easter Eggs

It's Spring! It's Easter!
And you know what that means...
Time for colored eggs
And cherry jelly beans.

I help Mama boil the eggs.
We let them cool and dry.
We get the colors ready,
Then drop them in the dye.

We use lots of lively colors
To dye the eggs real bright.
Yellow, green, pink, and blue –
Such a pretty sight!

Some we paint with stripes,
On some, we write a name,
Some we paint with polka-dots,
And some we paint the same.

Mama says I am a big help
And, because I am so sweet,
She likes to reward me
With a chocolate bunny treat.

It takes time to color eggs
But now our job is done...
Tomorrow is the Easter Egg Hunt
And I'll have tons of fun!

Can't Make Up My Mind

I'm hungry for some ice cream.

What flavor would be best?

I wish that they would let me take a taste test.

Vanilla, chocolate, strawberry

Chocolate mint chip

Butter pecan, raspberry

Vanilla chocolate twist

Bubble gum, peanut butter, pistachio

Rocky road, fudge ripple, chocolate marshmallow

I would really like to get a scoop of every kind.

What should I do? I can't make up my mind.

Big Barney

I love Big Barney!
His body, round and fat,
He wears a curly orange wig
And an orange and yellow hat.

His face is painted white,
He has a black rubber nose.
He wears a purple tie
With polka-dotted clothes.

His lips are ruby red,
His eyebrows are green,
And he has the biggest smile
That you've ever seen.

He blows up balloons,
He tells funny jokes,
He drives a crazy car
And breaks all the spokes.

I love Big Barney!
He's such a funny clown.
He makes me so happy.
I'm glad he came to town.

Circus

The big tent is up,
The crowd is coming,
Young people, old people –
The band is humming!

The ring master announces
The trapeze artist pair
Sailing hundreds of feet
Through the air.

The strong man lifts 300 pounds
Over his head
As elephants roll over,
Pretending to be dead.

Lions leap through
Blazing hoops of fire,
While acrobats do flips,
Going higher and higher.

Bareback riders on horses
Do stunts up and down
While children laugh and clap
At the tricks of a clown.

The crowd oohs and aahs,
The circus comes to a close
As a fat funny juggler
Spins plates on his nose.

CPSIA information can be obtained
at www.ICGtesting.com
Printed in the USA
LVHW071249090221
678819LV00017B/195